W9-BCT-417

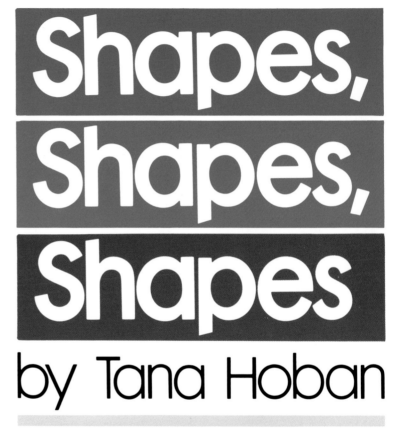

Shapes, Shapes, Shapes

by Tana Hoban

Greenwillow Books  New York

Shapes, Shapes, Shapes
Copyright © 1986
by Tana Hoban
All rights reserved.
Manufactured in China.
For information address
HarperCollins Children's
Books, a division of
HarperCollins Publishers,
10 East 53rd Street,
New York, NY 10022.
www.harperchildrens.com
First Edition
13 SCP 20 19 18 17 16 15 14 13

Library of Congress
Cataloging-in-Publication Data
Hoban, Tana.
Shapes, shapes, shapes.
"Greenwillow Books."
Summary:
Photographs of familiar
objects such as chair,
barrettes, and manhole cover
present a study of rounded
and angular shapes.
1. Geometry—Juvenile literature.
(1. Shape—Pictorial works.
2. Geometry—Pictorial works)
I. Title.
QA447.H631986
516.2'15   85-17569
ISBN 0-688-05832-9 (trade)
ISBN 0-688-05833-7 (lib. bdg.)
ISBN 0-688-14740-2 (pbk.)

The photographs were reproduced
from 35-mm slides and printed in full color.
The typeface is Avant Garde.

8116

for my mother

"And all that's best of dark and bright
 Meet in her aspect and her eyes."—Lord Byron

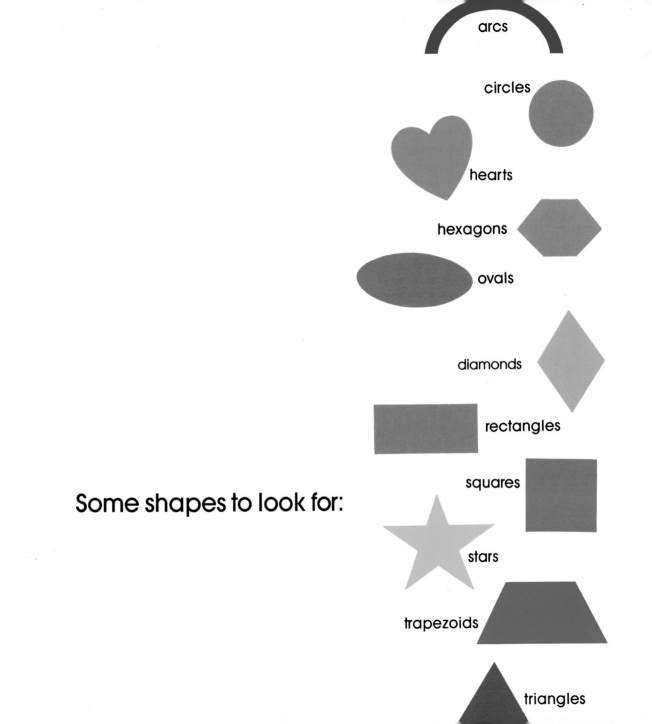

arcs

circles

hearts

hexagons

ovals

diamonds

rectangles

squares

Some shapes to look for:

stars

trapezoids

triangles

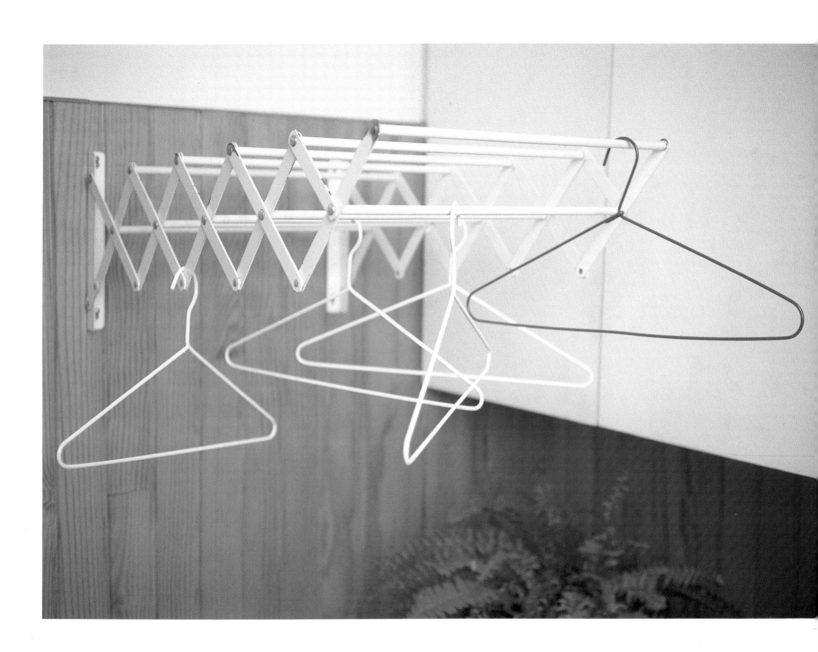